The Sun is Up!

by Sascha Goddard

OXFORD
UNIVERSITY PRESS

Mum and Dad get up.

The sun is up.

ram

A ram runs to the pen.

The rams go into the pen.

A carrot is in the mud.

carrot

Mum digs the carrots up.

egg

Dad picks up the eggs.

The duck is in the muck.

The duck pecks.

It is sunset.